THE *Almost*
EMPTY NESTER

REFLECTION JOURNAL

Your Essential Companion to
The Almost Empty Nester Book

The Almost Empty Nester Reflection Journal:
Your Essential Companion to *The Almost Empty Nester* Book
Copyright © 2024 Karla Olson

Requests for permission should be addressed to storybuilderspress@gmail.com
Published by StoryBuilders Press

Printed Journal: 978-1-954521-58-2
Digital: 978-1-954521-57-5

CONTENTS

INTRODUCTION

Welcome! I am overjoyed you purchased this companion guide for the *Almost Empty Nester.* This reflective journal was crafted to be a personal space for you to thoughtfully expand on the questions posed in the book. These exercises are meant to act as a compass to your soul whispers. They show you how to find your way back to your previous passions and direct you forward into a brand-new future that you are going to start creating now.

The *Almost Empty Nester* and this journal are divided into the following three sections to help you discover what's possible for you in this next phase of your life:

 THE PAST: *Take a moment to pause and reflect on what you've created. It's amazing, and it's a lot.*

 THE PRESENT: *Evaluate and honor where you are today. This is a good time to take inventory and rediscover your interests.*

 THE FUTURE: *Define what you want for your Empty Nesting years. Take time to dream, create a plan, and design how you're going to do it.*

This journal will inspire you to uncover your hopes and dreams for the next phase of your life. The reflection exercises are here to provide you clarity, insight, and self-awareness. Take what resonates with you and set aside the rest. There's no pressure to answer everything all at once—some questions may speak to you later, or not at all, and that is perfectly fine. Trust your instincts, focus on what feels important, and let's start creating your next best chapter.

And, by the way, if someone hasn't told you in a while, you're an incredible mom. I think you're amazing, and I'm so glad you are here.

xoxo,

Karla

SECTION I

The Past

CHAPTER 1

Hello, Stranger! Where Have You Been?

Coming home to yourself is the most important journey you'll ever take. It's where you'll find your heart, your courage, your voice, your compass, your joy, your authenticity.

—JENNIFER LOUDEN

I'm proud of you for acknowledging just how busy you've been raising children for the last fifteen to twenty-plus years. As the pace of your daily life begins to shift, it's time to get comfortable with putting some of that love back into yourself. Your dreams and goals are truly valuable and absolutely worth achieving.

For your first exercise, I invite you to take a moment to reflect on the questions below. It's important to take inventory of where you are right now in your life so you can build upon your answers as you move through each exercise in this Reflection Journal.

What are my thoughts and beliefs about Empty Nesting?

_____

_____

_____

_____

_____

_____

_____

_____

How have I shown up for myself alongside being a present and engaged mom?

_____

_____

_____

_____

_____

_____

What are some personal dreams I set aside over the years for the sake of others?

_____

_____

_____

_____

_____

_____

What are some new skills I want to learn at this stage of my life?

_____

_____

_____

_____

_____

_____

What makes me excited to get up in the morning?

_____

_____

_____

_____

_____

What activities light me up from within and make me lose track of time?

_____

_____

_____

_____

_____

_____

What do I want to experience in this next phase of my life?

_____

_____

_____

_____

_____

_____

_____

As you close your journal and set down your pen, remember that reflecting on these questions and answering each of them honestly is an important first step towards understanding and embracing your Empty Nest Dream.

I want every
talented, amazing
mother and soon to
be Empty Nester
to fall in love with
her future.

CHAPTER 2

What to Expect During Empty Nesting
Learning to Thrive

Give the ones you love wings to fly, roots to come back, and reasons to stay.

—THE DALAI LAMA

As you begin to reframe how you think about Empty Nesting, it's time to connect with your younger self. You were once a new mother, facing a future of hopes, dreams, and a lot of unknowns—and you're about to be in that space again as your children leave the nest. Today, you're going to connect with that new mom you once were and let her know how much she's grown.

Find a special photo of you when you first became a mother, whether it's one from the day your child was born or your first Mother's Day. Look at that precious picture, and really connect with that younger version of yourself.

Describe what it was like holding your newborn for the first time.

_____

_____

_____

_____

_____

_____

_____

_____

_____

What was going through your mind at that moment?

_____

_____

_____

_____

_____

_____

_____

How would you explain to her the incredible journey she is about to embark on?

_____

_____

_____

_____

_____

_____

_____

What would you want her to know?

_____

_____

_____

_____

_____

_____

_____

You've come so far since the day you became a mother. It's now time to reflect on and take pleasure in the life you've so lovingly built for yourself and your family over the years. Take a minute to write her a letter and connect to your younger self. To the young mother version of me:

What kind of mother did you hope to be?

- *Tell your younger self what kind of mother you have become.*

Can you believe how much you know now versus then?

- *Tell her how much you've learned to instill her with excitement, confidence, and faith for her future.*

What scared you most as a new mom?

- *Tell her how it all worked out or how you got through some difficult times because of her strength.*

What were your dreams for your family?

- *Tell her about some of the incredible dreams that came true.*

What would you want to tell her about her children and who they have become today?

- *Tell her about her amazing little humans that she gets to share her love, life, and wisdom with.*

What kind of struggles are coming her way?

- *Tell her about a few bumps in the road and how she got through them with grit and grace.*

What's the most important thing you want to tell this younger version of yourself?

- *Give her a "North Star nugget"—one incredibly powerful thing she can hold on to forever.*

***Thank her** for how she showed up every day, how much love she gave and continues to give, and how much she has grown as a woman.*

***Forgive her** for not being perfect (there's no such thing), and applaud her efforts to be the best mom she could be.*

Letter to My Younger Self

_____
_____
_____
_____
_____
_____
_____
_____
_____
_____
_____
_____
_____
_____
_____
_____
_____
_____
_____
_____
_____
_____

By writing this letter to the "beautiful, brand-new mother" version of yourself, you are bridging the gap between her dreams of yesterday and your present self. This reflection and introspection are reminders of the transformative power you possess and the immense strength you've carried through the ebbs and flows of motherhood. It's a celebration of growth, resilience, and the unique, beautiful bond between a woman of yesterday and the extraordinary mother you are now. It's a testament to your powerful, unique journey.

Find joy amidst
the pain—look for
the glimmers.

CHAPTER 3

Your Highlight Reel
Time to Shine

Motherhood is a collection of countless small moments that add up to a lifetime
of love, sacrifice, and joy. It's your beautiful, unique masterpiece.

—**UNKNOWN**

Highlight reels are so important to have as we head into our Empty Nesting years. It's important to look back before we move forward. It's time to really soak up what has transpired over the past fifteen to twenty plus years. It's amazing, and it's a lot! You have created so many beautiful memories for your family. Write down as much as you can about your journey as a mother. Remember, don't focus on your kids' accomplishments right now. Yes, those are extremely important, but let's focus on you. I invite you to think about these questions as you put together your personal Mom Highlight Reel.

What have you enjoyed most about raising your children?

_____

_____

_____

_____

_____

_____

_____

_____

What are you most proud of?

_____

_____

_____

_____

_____

_____

_____

What memories pop into your head that are priceless?

_____

_____

_____

_____

_____

_____

_____

What memories make you laugh out loud?

_____

_____

_____

_____

_____

_____

_____

What have you learned?

_____

_____

_____

_____

_____

_____

_____

What have you personally overcome, and what did that teach your children?

_____

_____

_____

_____

_____

_____

_____

What environment did you create for your children to grow up in?

_____

_____

_____

_____

_____

_____

What obstacles did you work through together, and how did this make your family stronger?

_____

_____

_____

_____

_____

What values are most important to you?

_____

_____

_____

_____

_____

_____

What are your best attributes as a mother?

_____

_____

_____

_____

_____

Spend some time going through pictures, albums, or journals if you have them. Reminisce. Look at how young you were and how far you've come! Take some time to enjoy this process because you deserve it. You've done such an amazing job with your little humans, and you need to know that on a soul level.

Magical mini moments make a lifetime of beautiful memories.

CHAPTER 4

Little Moments are Big Moments
Make Time to Dance in the Rain

When you dance, your purpose is not to get to a certain place on the dance floor; it's to enjoy each step along the way.

—WAYNE DYER

It's time to give yourself the gift of hearing from your children and what they love most about you. It's okay if you feel some big emotions as you work through these. It's a profound experience to get honest and loving feedback from your children. Their answers will probably make you laugh and cry. Enjoy this, Mama. You've earned it.

Chat with your children to uncover some of their favorite memories of you and what truly matters to them. No matter how old they are, ask them. As you look at the list, feel free to come up with your own questions to add. Make sure to record their answers in some way so you can keep them forever.

What's one of your favorite planned or unplanned memories of us together?

_____

_____

_____

_____

_____

_____

_____

_____

What's one thing I did when you were little that made you feel loved?

_____

_____

_____

_____

_____

What's your favorite family tradition?

_____

_____

_____

_____

_____

What's one thing I do that makes you laugh?

_____

_____

_____

_____

_____

_____

What's your favorite meal I make?

_____

_____

_____

_____

_____

_____

What's your favorite thing we have done and continue to do together?

_____

_____

_____

_____

_____

_____

What's one thing you loved doing together that you think I might not remember?

_____

_____

_____

_____

_____

_____

What's one of the best things I have taught you?

_____

_____

_____

_____

_____

_____

_____

_____

What do you love most about me?

_____

_____

_____

_____

_____

_____

_____

_____

_____

Your love for them has been unwavering, and it will continue as they embark on their own journey. Remember, you will always be their mother. Take a moment to pause and really take in how much you've inspired and influenced your kids over the years with your endless love, humor, kindness, and compassion. It truly is remarkable.

We have the power to impact our children in ways they will remember for a lifetime, and this doesn't end when they move out of the house.

CHAPTER 5

Your Old Toolbox
Out With the Old, In With the New

Without letting go of the old, it is impossible to make room for the new.

—DEEPAK CHOPRA

Take a moment to assess if your go-to "tools" are working for you in a positive and uplifting manner or not. Some tools you have may be working well, and some might be holding you back. Let's define and refine them before you head into your Empty Nesting years. It's time for a little tune-up.

Let's do some internal housekeeping, or "soul-keeping" as I like to call it, to better understand how you've been showing up in your everyday life.

Is life currently working out the way you want it to, or do you have some things you would like to change?

_____

_____

_____

_____

_____

_____

_____

_____

What beliefs and behaviors have you internalized over the years that are now automatic thoughts and habits stuck on rinse and repeat?

_____

_____

_____

_____

_____

_____

_____

_____

What do you need to let go of before you create your Empty Nest life?

_____

_____

_____

_____

_____

_____

_____

_____

Some of the tools you've been using could be outdated and no longer serving you in a positive way. Identify which ones used to work for you but now feel inauthentic as you've grown older and wiser. Heading into this next chapter of life is a good time to consciously choose what to keep and what to replace. Choose tools that better align with who you are today. Let's reorganize your toolbox. Start with the easy part: What needs to go? I invite you to make a list of every tool that no longer serves you and take it out of your toolbox. As you list them, consider how you've used them in the past and why they no longer serve you. Knowing why you were using them will help you not pick those old tools back up again. This isn't a time for blaming or shaming yourself for those old, not-so-great tools. We all have tools that need to go.

WRITE DOWN A LIST OF TOOLS YOU ARE GOING TO THROW OUT AND WHY.

- _____
- _____
- _____
- _____
- _____
- _____
- _____
- _____
- _____

Next, envision your brand-new toolbox. It's beautiful and shiny, with no marks on it. It hasn't felt the weight of pain or disappointment. It contains nothing except what you're about to put into it. What tools are you going to keep that are currently working well, and what brand-new tools are you going to add? This is the toolbox you will be taking into your future, so think big. Your brain will seek out what you focus on. If you're having trouble thinking of some new power tools, think of people you love and the qualities you admire about them. Write those down. Chances are, those are tools you want to develop in yourself, so add them to your toolbox.

WRITE DOWN A LIST OF TOOLS YOU ARE GOING TO KEEP.

- _____
- _____
- _____
- _____
- _____
- _____
- _____
- _____
- _____
- _____

WRITE DOWN A LIST OF *NEW* TOOLS YOU ARE GOING TO ADD. WITH MY NEW TOOLS I...

- _____
- _____
- _____
- _____
- _____
- _____
- _____
- _____
- _____
- _____
- _____
- _____
- _____

Taking time now to assess what is and isn't working for you will have a great impact on your next chapter in life. Empty Nesting can be viewed as a fresh start, a great time to check in with yourself and intentionally identify what you want more or less of in life.

When you start replacing your old tools with some new ones, your brain might try to trick you into returning back to your original state. That's just the brain doing its thing. When this happens (and it will), do these four things immediately so you don't return to your old habit loop: Recognize. Acknowledge. Replace. Repeat.

Recognize that the old behavior showed up.

Acknowledge why it showed up.

Replace it with something out of your new toolbox.

Repeat. Repeat. Repeat.

Now, let's put your new tools to work!

So many middle aged mothers are awakening to their individuality, finding their true voice, and rediscovering their unique passions and purpose.

CHAPTER 6

The Payoff of Courage vs. The Price of Regret
It's Time to Get into the Arena

Life shrinks or expands in proportion to one's courage.

—ANAIS LIN

Reflecting on the payoff of courage versus the price of regret can be a transformative exercise. Consistently choosing courage over time can have a profound impact on all areas of your life, as it compounds with each act of bravery. It sets you on a path of growth, resilience, and fulfillment. Let's reflect for a moment on courage and what acts of bravery have defined your path. How has courage propelled you forward, and how has not being courageous held you back?

Describe a particular moment in your life when you felt fulfilled for being courageous.

_____

_____

_____

_____

_____

_____

_____

_____

_____

_____

When have you experienced fear when doing something new, but you did it anyway?

_____

_____

_____

_____

_____

_____

_____

In what areas of your life do you feel you could have been more courageous?

_____

_____

_____

_____

_____

_____

_____

Where do you see an opportunity to be courageous right now?

_____

_____

_____

_____

_____

_____

_____

What do you regret not taking courageous action on in the past, and why do you regret it?

_____

_____

_____

_____

_____

_____

_____

_____

Think about a time when you witnessed someone else's act of courage. How did it inspire or impact you to do the same?

_____

_____

_____

_____

_____

_____

_____

_____

_____

_____

_____

Take a moment to review your answers and embrace the lessons they hold. For in the end, one true measure of our worth lies not in the absence of fear but in the courage we choose to act on.

Tune into your inner voice, trust your instincts, and define your next chapter with courage.

CHAPTER 7

Accept That Change is Coming
Empty Nesting is Right Around the Corner

Step into the new story you are willing to create.

—OPRAH WINFREY

By embracing the reality that your children are growing up and starting to move out, you will begin to shift your energy from a place of resistance to a place of acceptance. This new perspective allows you to approach Empty Nesting with a focus on proactive preparation while fostering a greater sense of excitement, hope, and peace.

Congratulations on completing Section One of the Reflection Exercises. I'm so proud of you for reviewing your past with an open heart, allowing yourself time to reflect on your achievements and how far you've come, cleaning out your toolbox, and even hearing from your children. Whew, that's a lot to unpack, and if you're anything like me, this experience involved some big emotions.

Take a few minutes to reread your answers (and your children's) from the previous exercises. By having this fresh in your mind, you will be better able to apply the lessons ahead.

During this phase of your life, your emotions will ebb and flow. On the more difficult days, as you reflect on your time with your kids, remember to embrace those moments when thinking about your PAST:

Parenting is a profound journey for everyone.
Acknowledge the beautiful moments.
Separate yourself from your mistakes.
Trust that incredible opportunities await.

Section Two of the Reflection Exercises is all about your present life, your thoughts and beliefs, identifying your current passions, and believing in yourself. Starting something fresh in mid-life can be so exciting, and that's what this next section is all about. You are doing great. Let's press on.

There's so much power in accepting your reality.

SECTION II

Present

CHAPTER 8

Clear the Canvas
Fresh Starts Can Feel So Good

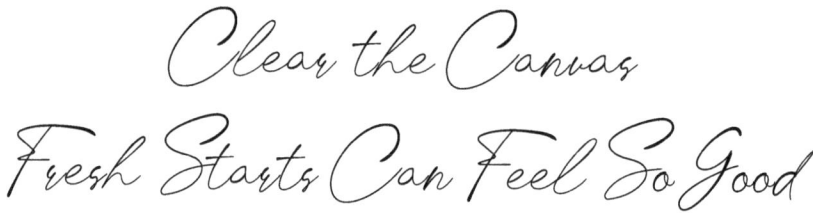

Sunsets are proof that endings can often be beautiful too.

—BEAU TAPLIN

There is power in starting something fresh in mid-life with the wisdom you've gained over the years. Let's picture your blank canvas for a moment as two giant jigsaw puzzles. One is full with your current commitments. The other puzzle is incomplete for the moment, but soon we will fill it up. When you think about the first puzzle, your current life, what do you spend most of your waking hours doing? How many priorities (pieces) does it have? Does it stress you out or bring you peace? Rank the pieces by importance—big, medium, and small.

In this next phase of your life, some pieces will stay the same, be removed, and may become larger or smaller based on their importance. This exercise allows you to visualize the amount of space that will open up for you as your children start to leave the nest and what you can do with that extra time.

As you answer the reflection questions, think about your current, completely full puzzle (and I bet it's jam-packed!).

 What responsibilities take up the most space in your day?

- ○ *Is it work, taking care of the children, activities, managing the household, working out, cooking, cleaning, etc.?*
- ○ *Make sure to list what the obvious big ones are, followed by the medium and small ones.*

_____

_____

_____

_____

Which responsibilities will decrease as your children start to move out?

_____

_____

_____

_____

_____

_____

_____

_____

_____

_____

_____

_____

What puzzle piece is going to fall off that you really enjoy doing?

_____

_____

_____

_____

_____

_____

How can you add something similar back in to replace it?

_____

_____

_____

_____

_____

If one of the puzzle pieces you personally love to do has shrunk, how can you make it bigger?

_____

_____

_____

_____

_____

_____

_____

Taking time to focus on what you love about your life right now and what's about to change is important.

When you look at your puzzle pieces all together, does it create a beautiful picture of the life you want?

_____

_____

_____

_____

_____

_____

How can you adjust your priorities to add more joy into your life?

_____

_____

_____

_____

_____

_____

_____

_____

_____

Which pieces are most important to you as you head into your Empty Nesting years?

_____

_____

_____

_____

_____

_____

_____

_____

_____

_____

_____

_____

Which pieces do you need to take out completely?

_____

_____

_____

_____

_____

_____

_____

_____

_____

_____

_____

_____

_____

_____

_____

_____

_____

You've poured a lot of love into creating this beautiful life of yours, so I want you to add the things you love into your new, unfinished puzzle, which is your blank canvas for your Empty Nest Life. This is an important part of the book because your future can look any way you want it to. It really can! I hope all your wishes and dreams make it onto your new blank canvas. Let's take a quick look at what you believe is possible for your Empty Nesting years and make sure you are dreaming big enough before you create your next best chapter.

MY BRAND NEW EMPTY NEST CANVAS

Empty Nesting is a blank canvas awaiting your artistic touch.

CHAPTER 9

Thoughts and Beliefs
Declutter Your Mind to Harness the Power Within

Your thoughts and beliefs shape your reality, for when you change your mind, you change your life.

—DR. JOE DISPENZA

Now that you understand how thoughts and beliefs create your feelings, actions, and experiences, you can fine tune them to align with your true purpose and desired outcomes.

By diving deep into any limiting beliefs you have, you will gain valuable insight into the stories you tell yourself and the impact they have on your life. Recognizing the duration of these thoughts, their origins, and their relevance in your present reality allows you to separate yourself from the burden of your outdated narratives.

Write down the limiting beliefs and negative thoughts you currently have running on repeat.

_____

_____

_____

_____

_____

_____

_____

_____

_____

How long have you had these thoughts?

_____

_____

_____

_____

_____

When did they start and why?

_____

_____

_____

_____

_____

_____

_____

Are these true for you today, or are they old stories?

_____

_____

_____

_____

_____

_____

_____

Did they start with you or someone else? Take the time to explain their origins if you can remember them.

_____

_____

_____

_____

_____

What have these limitations prevented you from achieving?

_____

_____

_____

_____

_____

_____

What are you willing to do about it today?

_____

_____

_____

_____

_____

_____

It's okay if a lot comes up. You've been alive for many years, my friend. But let's make sure these limiting beliefs don't follow you into your Empty Nest. Now, take a minute and FLIP each one of your negative beliefs into a more positive narrative. FLIP stands for Feel Like It's Possible. Whenever a limiting belief pops into your head, FLIP it and write down the exact positive opposite. Do this for every limiting belief you have. Clearing away these limitations opens up new possibilities and paves the way for your personal growth.

_____

_____

_____

_____

_____

_____

_____

_____

_____

_____

_____

_____

_____

_____

_____

_____

Heading into this next chapter of your life with these cobwebs cleared out will allow you to create your new passion project from a clearer point of view. How refreshing is that?!

Break free from
unconscious patterns and
create positive change
in your life.

CHAPTER 10

The Ten Cs
The Path to Your Purpose

The only way to do great work is to love what you do. If you haven't found it yet, keep looking, and don't settle. As with all matters of the heart, you'll know when you find it.

—STEVE JOBS

Let's go through a self-discovery exercise I call the Ten Cs. It's the heart and foundation of this book. The Ten Cs are ten words to reflect on to help you discover your current passions and interests. Don't worry, you don't have to make a really long list. But do write down a few thoughts for each word as they come to mind. Creating your Ten Cs list can give you a greater sense of what you want to create in this next chapter of life.

CONNECTION

○ *What are you deeply connected to in your life? This could be a person/place/thing.*

_____

_____

_____

_____

_____

_____

_____

_____

CONVERSATION

- What do you find yourself always conversing about? You can talk about this for hours.

_____

_____

_____

_____

_____

CHALLENGE

- What challenges do you enjoy? Or have you overcome something where sharing your story might benefit others?

_____

_____

_____

_____

_____

COMPASSION

- What brings out your compassion? What pulls at your heartstrings?

_____

_____

_____

_____

_____

CONTRIBUTION

o   *How do you like to contribute to those around you? In what ways do you like to make a difference?*

_____

_____

_____

_____

_____

CONVICTION

o   *What are you convicted about? What is at the core of your belief system?*

_____

_____

_____

_____

_____

_____

CURIOSITY

o   *What are you curious about? What has always piqued your interest?*

_____

_____

_____

_____

_____

CREATIVITY

o   *What kind of creative outlets do you enjoy? What is something new you want to learn?*

_____

_____

_____

_____

_____

COMMUNITY

o   *What does community mean to you? How do you like to make an impact?*

_____

_____

_____

_____

_____

CELEBRATION

o   *What do you love to celebrate about life? What brings you joy?*

_____

_____

_____

_____

_____

After you went through the Ten Cs questions, were you surprised by any of your answers that bubbled up? What themes do you see? Were old ones making their way to the surface? Which ones resonate with you the most?

_____

_____

_____

_____

_____

_____

_____

_____

_____

_____

_____

_____

_____

_____

_____

_____

_____

_____

_____

_____

For now, go back to your list and circle your Top Five that repeatedly made the list. It doesn't mean you won't get to the others, but we want to see which five are rising to the top. If you have a clear number one, circle it. That's great. If you have five, that's great too. Next, think about the things you circled and how they would impact the following areas of your life:

- *Your personal happiness and health*

- *Your marriage or partnership*

- *Your children*

- *Friends and family*

- *A new audience that may need your service or story*

- *Your community*

- *Your finances*

It's a good use of your time every few months or so to check back in with yourself and revisit your Ten Cs. That way, you can ensure whether you are on track in your day-to-day life and putting time into what you love, or if you have gotten off course and need to change direction.

Your priorities will continue to evolve and shift over time. And, by staying in tune with that, you can make sure you're focusing on the things that matter most to you.

When you ask deeper questions you get better answers.

CHAPTER 11

Your One Thing
What Lights You Up?

Whatever you do, or dream you can do, begin it. Boldness has genius, power, and magic in it.

—JOHANN WOLFGANG VON GOETHE

Picking your One Thing may feel uncomfortable at first, but I want you to trust this process, and do it anyway. Let's pick your One Thing right now. Don't overthink it, just do it. Go with your gut. Close your eyes, and say the very first one that comes to mind out loud. Write it down, and sit with it for a few minutes. You can always come back and change it later, but for now let's assume this is your number-one choice. Would spending time on this make you extremely happy? If so, then that is the one you should pick. Time is your most valuable currency, so plan to use it doing what you love.

Focusing on your One Thing can initiate a cascade of transformative benefits that will positively impact many aspects of your life. Write down the ways you envision your life changing for the better if you stick with your One Thing and really give it your best shot.

What new disciplines will you develop?

_____

_____

_____

_____

_____

_____

_____

How will it feel to cultivate determination and grit in the pursuit of this endeavor?

_____

_____

_____

_____

_____

_____

_____

Who in your life will be affected in a positive way seeing you work on your passion project?

_____

_____

_____

_____

_____

_____

_____

How could it have a domino effect in your life?

_____

_____

_____

_____

_____

_____

_____

How will you feel when you wake up in the morning?

_____

_____

_____

_____

_____

_____

What are some new things you can talk about with friends and family?

_____

_____

_____

_____

_____

_____

By working on your One Thing, how do you see it leading you to eventually working on your other soul whispers?

_____

_____

_____

_____

_____

_____

The act of picking your One Thing and cultivating it creates a powerful effect, ushering in a renewed sense of purpose, self-discovery, and personal growth. It's the perfect place to be when you start planning for what you want in your Empty Nesting years. Nice job!

Trust yourself and stick with the choice that is naturally bubbling up to the top.

CHAPTER 12

Inner Critic vs Inner Compass
Busting Through the BS to
Discover Your True North

I deeply believe that each one of us has an inner compass that points us
towards our true north, and if we have the courage to listen and follow it, we
can navigate our way to a life of authenticity, purpose, and joy.

—GLENNON DOYLE

Haven't listened to your Inner Compass in a while? Been listening to your Inner Critic too much? I hear you. Change can be scary—I get it. Once you understand that your Inner Critic is simply trying to keep you safe, you can move beyond it and start to seek the voice of your Inner Compass instead.

Oftentimes, you need to get outside of yourself to see what's truly possible. You need to squash those scarcity glasses today and adjust the lens with which you see the world to embrace your own uniqueness, unlimited potential, and incredible possibilities. You are the only one who gets to decide which of those Inner Critic thoughts or beliefs get left behind and which Inner Compass thoughts or beliefs will keep you on the right path forward.

Let's do that now. In the left column on the next page, make a list of what your Inner Critic is thinking about your new goals. On the right side, list everything your Inner Compass is thinking. Notice the major differences.

INNER CRITIC

_____

_____

_____

_____

_____

_____

_____

_____

_____

_____

_____

_____

_____

_____

_____

_____

_____

_____

INNER COMPASS

_____

_____

_____

_____

_____

_____

_____

_____

_____

_____

_____

_____

_____

_____

_____

_____

_____

_____

Now that you've created this list of your Inner Critic versus your Inner Compass, which would you rather listen to?

Listening to your Inner Compass is such a beautiful way to live, and it will rub off on your children in a positive way, too. When they observe you using more confident self-talk language, quieting your fears and doubts, and encouraging yourself more, they will start to do the same. Kick your Inner Critic to the curb, and commit to nurturing your Inner Compass from now on.

Write down your commitment here to always listen to your Inner Compass. From this day forward, I will...

_____

_____

_____

_____

_____

_____

_____

_____

_____

_____

_____

_____

_____

_____

_____

_____

_____

You were meant to
lead with your heart
and trust your gut.

CHAPTER 13

Lens of a Friend
Outside Perspective Can Be So Beautiful

Sometimes it takes the perspective of a friend to unveil the hidden possibilities within ourselves.

—UNKNOWN

Stepping outside of yourself is the beginning of changing the lens through which you see your world and all the possibilities waiting for you.

For this exercise, we're going to embody the energy of looking at your One Thing from the outside in. That's how you want to approach this—through the lens of your loving best friend.

Whoever is your biggest champion in life, I want you to embody that voice right now. That energy. That love. It took a lot of courage for you to pick your One Thing, so let's give you some encouragement and positive feedback from that outside perspective. Put your "bestie" glasses on as you work through these reflection questions.

Why does your One Thing seem like a great idea?

_____

_____

_____

_____

_____

_____

_____

_____

How will it fulfill you on a soul level?

_____

_____

_____

_____

_____

_____

_____

What possibilities do you envision for how this might actually work out?

_____

_____

_____

_____

_____

_____

_____

What does success look like for you?

_____

_____

_____

_____

_____

_____

_____

How can you encourage yourself to take the first action step despite not seeing the finish line?

_____

_____

_____

_____

_____

_____

When was the last time you did something for yourself just for the joy of it?

_____

_____

_____

_____

_____

_____

How will it feel knowing you are going to spend your time doing something you absolutely love to do?

_____

_____

_____

_____

_____

_____

Who would greatly benefit from you sharing your gifts?

_____

_____

_____

_____

_____

_____

_____

_____

_____

_____

_____

_____

_____

_____

_____

_____

I encourage you to be brave, get some feedback from trusted souls on your One Thing, and get started. You might get the unwavering support and valuable insight you've always needed. They might even ask you what your second or third thing was, and it can spark amazing insightful conversation. Please note, getting feedback is not asking for permission. You don't need permission from anyone else to go after your dreams. The feedback is meant to be a tool for you to gain insight into your strengths and anchor your belief that you can get there.

Having several trusted companions along the way who believe in your vision is so valuable. I want you to feel as excited and empowered as possible as you continue through the exercises in this book. You're doing great. Keep it up!

Commit to treating yourself as one of your very best friends for the rest of your life.

CHAPTER 14

It's Time to Take Action: Let's Get to Work!

The future belongs to those who believe in the beauty of their dreams.

—ELEANOR ROOSEVELT

By taking the time to review your past and assess where you are in the present, you are now prepared to create your next best chapter. This is the perfect opportunity to design the vibrant Empty Nest future you've always envisioned for yourself. Let's get to the good stuff. For the last exercise of Section Two, take a few minutes to reread your answers from Chapters 8-13. Having this insight and perspective fresh in your mind allows you to easily absorb and apply the framework taught in Chapters 14-21.

As you move toward a future filled with new opportunities, take a moment to be PRESENT:

Picture your blank canvas as symbolizing your new phase of life.

Rediscover your FLOW state moments.

Exchange each perceived limitation with a creative solution, and FLIP it.

Support yourself as you would a best friend.

Empower your future self by taking action now.

Nurture your One Thing, and visualize life once you've accomplished it.

Treat yourself with grace as you work through this process

Section 3 of this Reflection Journal is all about taking action and creating an amazing future for yourself, not tethered to the past, but aligned with a new destiny. Let's get crystal clear on how you want your life to look in the near future and make a plan to get there. Commit to yourself to see this next section through to the end. You'll be so glad you did. I'm excited for you and can't wait to witness your transformation!

By loving and nurturing your own needs alongside being a mother, you model positive behavior for your adult children.

SECTION III

Future

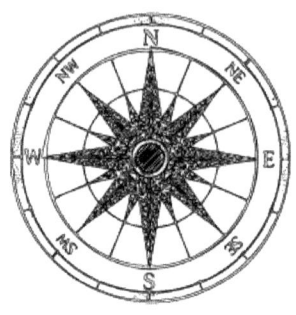

CHAPTER 15

Your Game Plan for Success
Action Is the Greatest Teacher

Making a plan for your dreams is the compass that guides you towards their realization.

—TONY ROBBINS

It's time to design an actionable game plan for achieving your One Thing. You will define the essential components, actionable steps, and SMART goals for your Empty Nest Game Plan. It will serve as a guiding blueprint for you that provides clarity, direction, and structure. Additionally, it's important to also get really clear on what a successful outcome means to you. Don't look outside yourself for this. Close your eyes, and visualize what your personal success outcome looks and feels like. It feels good, doesn't it?

Attach a powerful, positive emotion to your visualized outcome so you can really see it, feel it, and believe it! This is going to take some time, so please don't feel rushed. Work at a pace that is comfortable for you.

To get started, let's define your "Game Plan for Success" and apply some SMART goals to your plan: Specific. Measurable. Actionable. Realistic. Timely.

1. **Specific:**

   What exactly are you trying to accomplish? What is your One Thing you are working on? What is your desired outcome? Do you want to:

   - Get a new job?
   - Start a business?
   - Move to a new house or city?
   - Travel the world?
   - Prioritize self-care?
   - Learn a new skill or hobby?
   - Expand your friend group to include people who share your new interests?
   - Get your finances under control?
   - Go back to school?

These are all examples of noteworthy goals. I can't wait to hear about what you picked! I'm so excited for you. Please share in our community on all things social @TheEmptyNesterClub if you feel comfortable, and use the hashtag #OneThing or #GamePlan.

When your goals are specific, you can then take focused, intentional action. You are more likely to achieve the desired outcome when you get detailed with your goals.

_____

_____

_____

_____

_____

_____

_____

_____

_____

_____

_____

_____

_____

_____

_____

_____

_____

_____

_____

_____

2. Measurable:

How will you measure what you are doing? How will you assess your achievements?

Whatever your goal is, making it measurable will allow you to track your progress, make adjustments if necessary, and keep you motivated.

3. *Attainable:*

With the tools that you have, can you reach your goal? Is it doable? If not, what do you need to do in order to make it attainable?

Achieving small goals will boost your confidence and belief in your ability to accomplish larger goals in the future. This positive reinforcement is important for long-term success, so make sure your first goal is attainable.

4. *Realistic:*

What do you want to achieve by working on this One Thing, and are your expectations realistic? Can you meet the goals you defined for yourself based on your current level of knowledge, time available, and daily circumstances? Knowing why you want to achieve your goals will also help you get more clear on the how.

I love it when people dream big, but to achieve big dreams, you have to start small. Success is in the details. Big goals are realized when broken down into bite-sized baby steps taken consistently over time. Make sure your first goal is realistic, and build from there.

5. *Timely:*

What is the timeline to meet your goals? Work backward. Start with what date you want to achieve your goal by, and back into that date with your detailed plan. Create an outline for the milestones that need to be reached, and give them a date. This is one of the most important components of goal setting.

Backward planning helps you identify when each milestone needs to get done. When you attach a timeline to a goal, that will keep you on track and create a sense of urgency to achieve what you desire. You should be proud that you are going to take action on a dream you've had for a long time. Remember, start small so you can stack up some early successes. If you do that, you will be more consistent with your actions. I'm so excited to see what you create for yourself! You deserve it! Next, let's discuss how to get started in the right way so that you never want to quit ever again.

Your passions
are indeed worth
attaining.

CHAPTER 16

Baby Steps
Consistency Over Time Is Powerful

Consistency is the mother of mastery.

—ROBIN SHARMA

Let's infuse some new habits into your life today. Starting small can create a huge impact on your future with the right mindset. You're about to create a new way of building momentum without overwhelming yourself.

For this next exercise, I invite you to adopt a mindset that will be beneficial for this growth period: a flexible mindset. This will allow you to adapt to change as new information comes at you, which fosters innovation and progress. On the other hand, a rigid mindset resists change and often leads to missed opportunities for learning and improvement. So make sure you're going into this next process with a flexible mindset. Eighty percent is your new 100 percent, and adjustments are key for learning.

Make a list of the new, actionable baby steps you will take toward your game plan and SMART goals. Make sure they are bite-sized so you can ensure you'll do them and build your small wins. Remember, consistent effort over compounded time, not extra effort, leads to success. Pick one actionable step you will take today toward one small, attainable goal. Apply the "putting on your running shoes" concept to the first step you need to take for your desired result. Make sure you are aware of what you are currently craving because satisfying your current cravings will determine your success.

What's the one new goal or habit I will achieve today? And why is that important to me?

_____

_____

_____

_____

_____

_____

_____

_____

_____

What cue will I put into place to start this process?

○ **Cue:** *This is the trigger that initiates the behavior. It is a signal that prompts your brain to start a particular habit.*

_____

_____

_____

_____

_____

_____

_____

_____

_____

_____

What am I craving? Why did I pick this goal?

o **Craving:** *After the cue, there is a feeling of desire or craving, for the reward associated with the habit. This craving is what motivates you to act. Sidenote—craving novelty, excitement, or peaceful rest are three very different things, so make sure you know what your current needs are. Once you know what you need and crave in this moment, you can turn that baby step into success. This will allow you to maintain your new rhythm in life with much less effort.*

_____

_____

_____

_____

_____

_____

_____

What response will I have, and what will I do when I see my cue?

o **Response:** *This is the actual behavior or action that you will take in response to the cue. Make sure this is realistic, doable, and won't trigger alarms in your brain that think you are making too big of a change. Keep it small and simple.*

_____

_____

_____

_____

_____

_____

_____

_____

_____

What reward will I feel once I finish my new goal or habit?

- o **Reward:** *The reward is the outcome or benefit that you gain from performing the habit. It satisfies the craving and reinforces the habit loop.*

_____

_____

_____

_____

_____

_____

_____

_____

_____

_____

_____

_____

_____

_____

_____

_____

_____

By understanding and manipulating the four elements of a habit loop—the cue, craving, response, and reward—you can consistently and effectively build new habits or break old ones. Doing new things will cause your daily rhythms to change, and that's good. Change can feel threatening at first, but if you lean into it, stick with it, and consistently show up, it will positively affect your life in so many areas. Build on your baby steps, and celebrate your progress. It will help you maintain the new rhythm in life that you are creating for your best Empty Nest.

Make consistent, compounded effort toward your goal, and it will work for you. Every time.

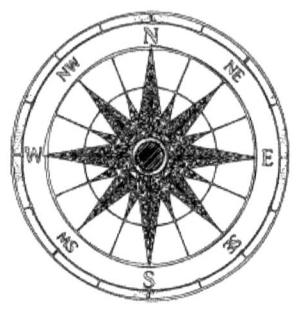

CHAPTER 17

Maintaining Your New Rhythm
Lean into the Discomfort

Embrace the discomfort of a new rhythm, for within it lies the potential for the most joyful transformation of your life.

—BRENÉ BROWN

It's so important to embrace this new rhythm in your life, especially when you are trying new things. You are working on new habits and goals, and that can feel unusual. But I promise after a little bit of time, it will start to feel normal. Lean into the discomfort for now, and keep going. One thing that I find helpful to do in case I feel myself slipping a bit is to interrupt the habit loop by adding one simple extra step: replacement.

Cue
Craving
Replacement
Response
Reward

Having a craving but not responding to it means something is up. The chain is disrupted somewhere. Adding in a temporary replacement (a placeholder if you will) can help you unlock the freeze and take action. That little replacement just might be enough to get you going and move you into response mode. Maybe you just needed a little push, and now you're ready to roll. Here's how you do this:

Identify resistance:

o   *How can you identify when you aren't following through on what you want and need to do, especially when you don't feel like doing it?*

_____

_____

_____

_____

_____

o   *What are the signs or signals that indicate you are resisting the new task or habit?*

_____

_____

_____

_____

_____

_____

o   *Is there a change in your habit loop, or do you just need a little push?*

_____

_____

_____

_____

_____

_____

_____

Questioning your beliefs:

o   *When faced with resistance or lack of motivation, tune into your internal dialogue. What questions can you ask yourself to challenge your resistance and reaffirm your commitment before you get too far off track?*

_____

_____

_____

_____

_____

Interrupting your habit loop:

o   *How can you interrupt the habit loop between craving and response? Insert a replacement behavior before your desired response. Consider a specific strategy or technique that can help you hijack your habit loop in just the right area.*

_____

_____

_____

_____

_____

o   *What new action can you introduce to shift your mindset and behavior towards fulfilling your commitment, even when you don't feel like it?*

_____

_____

_____

_____

 *SOS Model:*

    o   *What is something in your life that you can Stop, Offload, or Simplify that might help clear some things off your plate so you have a better chance of maintaining these new habits you have created?*

_____

_____

_____

_____

_____

_____

_____

    o   *What do you no longer need to do so you can open up space for new goals and habits?*

_____

_____

_____

_____

_____

_____

_____

_____

When you figure out how to lean into and maintain this new rhythm of life by hijacking your habits and applying the SOS model, you will be so happy you did as you start to see results. There are probably a lot of local communities you could tap into to keep your excitement and momentum going. It's great to go through this phase of life with like-minded friends in your community. Let's talk about the importance of finding that.

You are growing
forward and glowing up.

CHAPTER 18

Find Your Community Your Tribe Is Calling

Find your tribe. Love them hard. Together, you can create magic and manifest your shared vision.

—MEL ROBBINS

When you are working on creating momentum, having others who share your same interests can make such a positive difference in your life. Developing your Empty Nest community is a great way to connect with like-minded people who are experiencing the same phase in life.

For this exercise, spend some time researching groups within your community that are doing what you want to do. Who else is on the same journey as you, and how can you find them? If you can, hop online and see if there are any local meetup groups that share the same interests you have.

Additionally, call or email several friends and let them know you are soon to be an Empty Nester and would love to connect with other people they know who share your interests, both new and old. Maybe you are ready to finally write a book and share your own story. See if one of your friends can introduce you to an author who would be willing to have coffee with you. Or take your first Pickleball lesson. The possibilities are endless.

Ask yourself the following questions:

What's one way I could get to know more people in my community who share my interests?

_____

_____

_____

_____

_____

_____

_____

Who might need to connect with me that I don't know yet? How can I put myself out there?

_____

_____

_____

_____

_____

_____

Are any of these groups advertised in the local paper, library, or through a higher-ed school program?

_____

_____

_____

_____

_____

_____

If there's not a group, can I start up my own?

_____

_____

_____

_____

_____

_____

And most importantly, how can I best serve this new community?

_____

_____

_____

_____

_____

Make a list of a few ideas you have, and promise to take action on at least one or two. You will be glad you did.

_____

_____

_____

_____

_____

_____

When you find new friends you align with who are interested in the same things you are, it's almost as if the magic doubles.

CHAPTER 19

Future You
The Ripple Effect

Believe in the possibilities of creating an extraordinary future life for yourself, for it is within your power to make it a reality.

—ALBERT EINSTEIN

Let's start by imagining what your life looks like one year from now. No matter where you are on your Empty Nesting journey, just focus on the upcoming year. Let's also assume that you consistently worked on your One Thing over this past year.

Write down the date one year from today: _____.

Here's an opening sentence you could use to get the ball rolling: For the past year, I have worked on

_____

_____, and I cannot believe how much my life has changed!

Then answer these questions.

How are you showing up now that you have consistently worked on your One Thing? Like really knocked it out of the park?

_____

_____

_____

_____

_____

_____

Describe your ideal day. How has that improved?

_____

_____

_____

_____

_____

_____

Are you happier and braver? Less scattered or stressed?

_____

_____

_____

_____

_____

_____

_____

Do you wake up more excited than you used to be?

_____

_____

_____

_____

_____

_____

Are you lit up from within?

_____

_____

_____

_____

_____

_____

Are you attracting new people, places, experiences, and things into your life?

_____

_____

_____

_____

_____

_____

_____

What are you no longer doing or accepting?

_____

_____

_____

_____

_____

Describe, in detail, the ripple effect this has had in your life. How has this impacted you personally and those around you?

_____

_____

_____

_____

_____

_____

_____

Did you decide to work on other passion projects with newfound confidence and energy?

_____

_____

_____

_____

_____

_____

_____

What was your favorite part about this past year?

_____

_____

_____

_____

_____

What are you most proud of?

_____

_____

_____

_____

_____

_____

_____

_____

_____

_____

_____

_____

_____

_____

_____

Why one year? Because we overestimate what we can do in a day, but we underestimate what we can accomplish in a year. As you immerse yourself in this exercise, remember that the future version of you is not a distant entity but rather an intrinsic part of you waiting to be unleashed. She's always been in there, but now we're shining a bright light on her and bringing those gifts to the surface. Defining and embodying the qualities of your envisioned self will ignite a powerful force that propels you toward your desired future. Embrace this vision, nurture it, and let it guide you as you continue on this transformative journey of self-discovery and growth.

Future you is a rock star.

There is so much joy
in the journey.

CHAPTER 20

Celebrate and Serve
The Joy of Giving Back

True celebration and service go hand in hand, for in uplifting others,
we find the greatest joy and purpose within ourselves.

—OPRAH WINFREY

You have realigned yourself with a new purpose, crafted an exciting game plan for your Empty Nest years, and taken actionable baby steps towards a fulfilling future. Take time to celebrate yourself and all that you have accomplished so far. Additionally, consider that one of the best ways to celebrate is by serving and giving back to your community. For this exercise, reflect on what celebration and service mean to you. Answer the following questions.

CELEBRATION

How do you best like to celebrate your achievements, big or small?

_____

_____

_____

_____

_____

_____

_____

_____

How can you commit to celebrating yourself, even if you haven't in a while?

_____

_____

_____

_____

_____

_____

_____

In what ways can you mark this significant milestone in your life and honor your journey and growth?

_____

_____

_____

_____

_____

_____

_____

Reflect on the past accomplishments that you celebrated. How did those celebrations make you feel, and how can you replicate or enhance that feeling for your current achievements?

_____

_____

_____

_____

_____

_____

How can celebrating contribute to your overall well-being and motivate you to pursue future goals?

_____

_____

_____

_____

_____

_____

_____

It's no small feat you made it through all of the exercises in this journal, so plan yourself a great celebration!

SERVICE

When you think about service, answer these questions.

What causes or organizations deeply resonate with you and align with your values that you can contribute to in your Empty Nest years?

_____

_____

_____

_____

_____

_____

_____

_____

How can you leverage your skills, resources, or time to create a significant impact in the organizations or causes you are passionate about?

_____

_____

_____

_____

Reflect on a time when you contributed to a cause or an organization. How did that experience enrich your life, and how can you continue to integrate service into your Empty Nest journey?

_____

_____

_____

_____

_____

Who can you enroll to help you with this service? Is there a group of people you enjoy volunteering with?

_____

_____

_____

_____

Celebration and service are so important as you begin to wrap up this journey. Take some time to go back and read through your Reflection Exercises and take it all in. It's amazing what you have just accomplished, and I can't wait to see what the future holds for you.

As you reflect on your journey and growth, remember that celebrating your achievements and serving others are vital components of a fulfilling, purposeful life. Embrace the lessons learned, the perspectives gained, and the impact made as you move forward with renewed clarity and intention. The possibilities for your Empty Nest are endless, and I'm excited to witness the incredible transformation and success that lie ahead for you.

Empty Nesting is an ideal time to channel your passion and skills into endeavors that not only align with your values but benefit your community.

CHAPTER 21

A Final Letter to My Readers
I Believe in You

She remembered who she was and the game changed.

—LILAH DELIA

There is so much joy to be found in the Empty Nest journey. I know it can be hard when your babies start leaving the nest, but now you are prepared with a plan for what comes next, and that can be exhilarating. Take a moment to reflect on what you've learned and what you have designed for your Best Empty Nest!

Pause and express gratitude to the present you for taking the first steps towards your future dreams. Embrace this opportunity and let the wisdom and guidance you've learned along the way inspire and uplift you as you move forward. Here's to your bright FUTURE:

Follow your new game plan.

Utilize the power of SMART goals.

Take one step at a time.

Understand that success is about consistency, not perfection.

Roll with your One Thing and watch all the ripples that come from it.

Embrace a new tribe and find ways to serve your community.

For this last exercise, I invite you to write a heartfelt letter from your future self, with all that she has accomplished, to the mother you are today. Let this letter be a celebration of the progress you've made and a source of encouragement for the journey ahead. Express gratitude to the present you for taking the first steps toward your dreams. Embrace this opportunity, and let the wisdom and guidance of your future self inspire and uplift you.

Describe in detail every amazing new person, place, opportunity, or thing that has come into your life. Acknowledge the determination and resilience that brought you to where you are now. Embrace the excitement of the possibilities that lie before you. And be sure to thank the current you for having the clarity and courage to begin. You are an amazing gift to this world, and I am rooting for you!

Letter from My Future Self

You've been on an incredible journey throughout these twenty-one chapters. You embarked on a transformative path, rediscovered who you are before your kids leave the nest, and designed a future you can fall in love with. I want you to be immensely proud of the progress you've made. You've invested valuable time and energy in looking back at your journey as a mother. You've taken the courageous step of analyzing your current passions and identifying new projects that resonate with your Empty Nest plans. And you've taken actionable steps toward building your next best chapter. This introspection and work are a testament of your commitment to personal growth and self-discovery.

My wish for you is that you are proud of what you have accomplished in going through these exercises, entering your answers into this journal, and designing the future of your dreams. There is so much power and insight to be gained by taking a pause and reflecting on your motherhood journey, but also focusing on your future plans for yourself and designing your Empty Nest with intention. Thank you for being a part of this community, and I can't wait to witness your transformation. Please share what your #OneThing is over on @theemptynesterclub on all things social!

With heartfelt gratitude,
Karla

FINAL POEM TO MY READERS

The Gardener of Souls

In the garden of life, a mother sows,
Nurturing her children with love that flows,
Seeds of dreams, she carefully tends,
Watching her children bloom and ascend.
Proudly watch as they take to the skies
Spreading their wings while you dry your eyes.
You've loved and nurtured them so dearly.
You've done a great job. I mean this sincerely.
To the miracle mothers, the gardeners of souls,
Now that your nest is beginning to unfold,
It's time for you to blossom and bloom anew,
Rediscovering passion and dreams just for you.
There's joy to be found in this Empty Nest journey
It's important to start working on your future nest early.
Embrace this time and fall in love with your future.
The road will be less bumpy, and the ride much smoother.
Mothers deserve to feel fulfilled and bright,
Even as their children take off in flight.
It's time for women's gifts to be unfurled,
Together, we can illuminate and transform the world.
When women rise, we all climb higher
Awakening our souls to our internal fire
For in your heart, a universe resides,
Ready to bloom and conquer the tides.
So let your light shine, my dear miracle mother.
You're special indeed. You are like no other.
Gardeners of souls, with love's pure light,
I wish this next chapter to be one of the best in your life.